Do you Sudoku?
Book *for kids!*

Do you Sudoku?
Book *for kids!*

spinner/books

San Francisco • Maastricht • Sydney

Acknowledgments

Publisher: Bob Moog

Editor: Peter Crowell

Designer: Jeanette Miller

Special thanks to Erin Conley, Suzanne Cracraft, Elise Gresch and Kristen Schoen
for their invaluable assistance.

Spinner Books, a division of University Games Corporation
2030 Harrison Street San Francisco, CA 94110

University Games Europe B.V.
Australielaan 52 6199 AA Maastricht Airport, Netherlands

University Games Australia
10 Apollo Street Warriewood 2102 Australia

Library of Congress Cataloging-in-Publication Data on file with the publisher

ISBN: 1-57528- 963-6

Printed in Canada

1 2 3 4 5 6 7 8 9 10 - 09 08 07 06 05

Contents

Introduction

I've never really liked math, and I've never been much into number puzzles. That's always been the domain of my little brother Ricky. He could multiply three-digit numbers in his head when he was seven, and knew all sorts of tricks to dividing by 3 or 7 or something.

Boring!

But Sudoku is different. A Sudoku puzzle is a logic puzzle, not a number puzzle. It occurred to me that there might be others who get flustered by numbers, but enjoy logic. We experimented and discovered that by replacing the numbers in a Sudoku puzzle with letters or symbols, we eliminated any "number" anxiety. Then we took the puzzles to kids and received rousing applause. *Do You Sudoku? Book for kids!* was born. This book is really a great deal of fun - healthy fun. Our different puzzles will appeal to different parts of the brain. I like the *Symbolidoku* the best.

Now even seven-year-olds can join in the fun of Sudoku and build their brain power and logic muscles.

Have fun!

Bob

Rules

olving the puzzles:

et yourself a pencil with a fresh eraser! Now, look closely at the puzzle grid; it's divided
to six sections of six boxes each. To solve the Sudoku, fill in the blank spaces using
e figures in the key at the top of each puzzle. Make sure that **each six-box section**
ntains **one, and only one,** of the figures you're working with.

ut be careful!

u have to watch the whole grid, too. **Each row** in the whole grid must also have **one,
d only one,** of each figure. The same goes for **each column.**

our kinds of Sudoku!

ere are four kinds of Sudoku in this book. First there's *Symbolidoku,* that's Sudoku
ing symbols like moons and hearts. Next comes *Alphadoku,* that's Sudoku using letters
om the alphabet. Then there's *Geometridoku,* that's Sudoku using geometric shapes like
angles and squares. And finally there's *Numeridoku,* that's Sudoku using numbers.

**remember: Fill in each row, column AND six-box section with ONE, AND ONLY ONE,
the figures in the key.**

doku isn't easy, but it sure is simple!

Solve the puzzle by using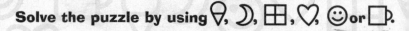

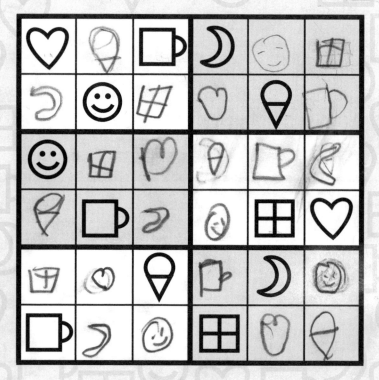

Solution on page 110

Solve the puzzle by using 𝖦, ☽, ⊞, ♡, ☺ or ⌷.

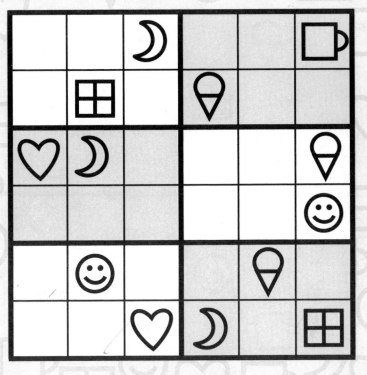

Solution on page 110

Solve the puzzle by using 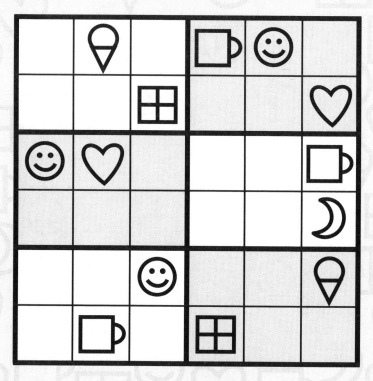, ☽, ⊞, ♡, ☺ **or** ⎚.

Solution on page 111

Solve the puzzle by using ♀, ☽, ⊞, ♡, ☺ or ☕.

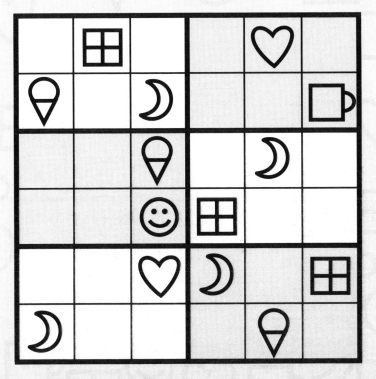

Solution on page 111

Solve the puzzle by using ⋒, ☽, ⊞, ♡, ☺ or ⬜.

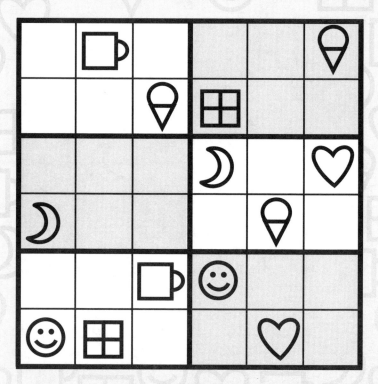

Solution on page 112

Solve the puzzle by using 🔻, 🌙, ⊞, 🤍, ☺ or 🍺.

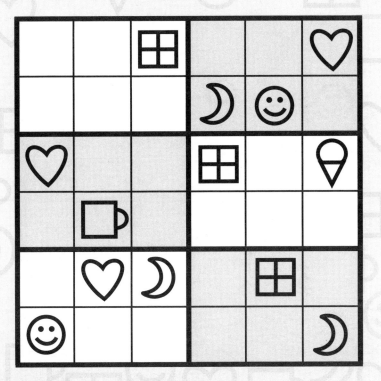

Solution on page 112

Solve the puzzle by using .

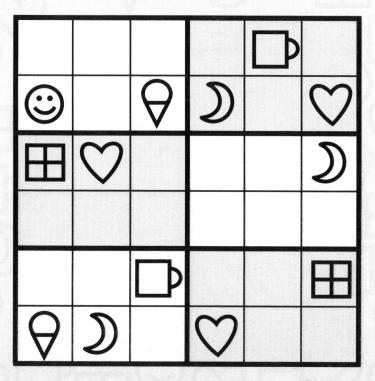

Solution on page 113

Solve the puzzle by using ♀, ☽, ⊞, ♡, ☺ or ☐.

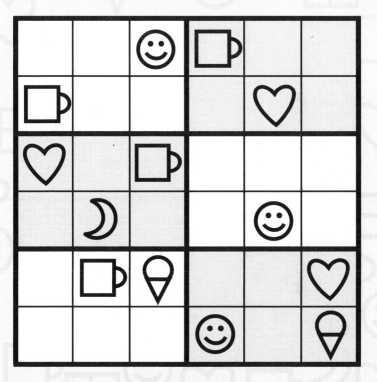

Solution on page 113

Solve the puzzle by using 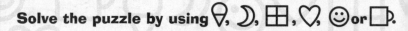.

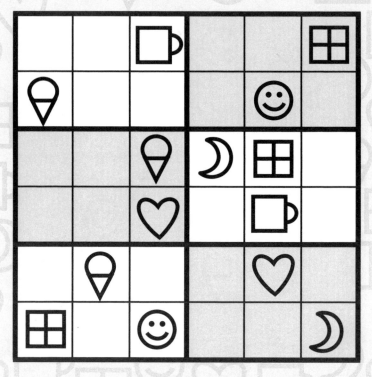

Solution on page 114

Solve the puzzle by using ♀, ☽, ⊞, ♡, ☺ or ⊐.

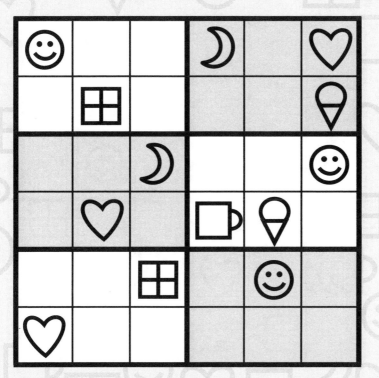

Solution on page 114

Solve the puzzle by using ♀, ☽, ⊞, ♡, ☺ or ⬛.

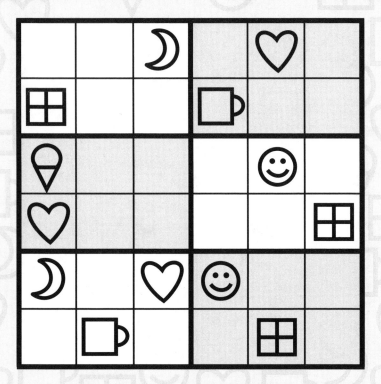

Solution on page 115

Solve the puzzle by using 🏮, 🌙, ⊞, ♡, ☺ or ☕.

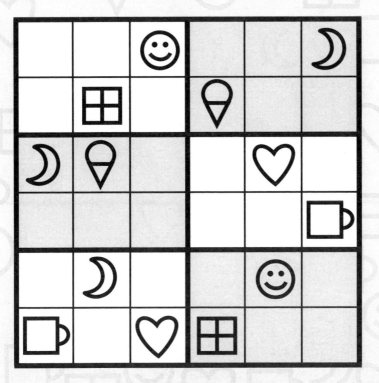

Solution on page 115

Solve the puzzle by using .

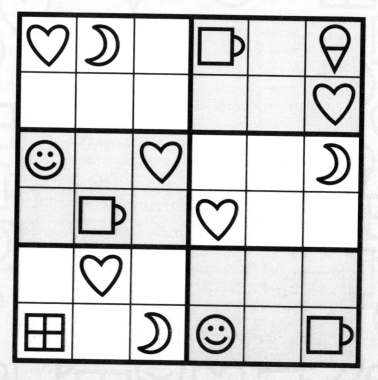

Solution on page 116

Solve the puzzle by using ♀, ☽, ⊞, ♡, ☺ or ⬓.

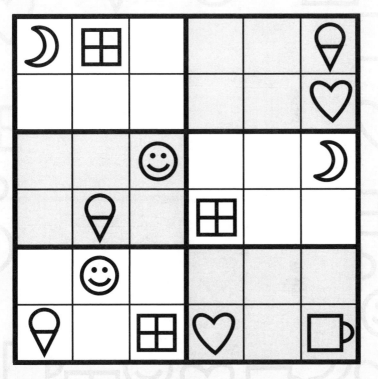

Solution on page 116

Solve the puzzle by using 𝒱,), ⊞, ♡, ☺ or ⬜.

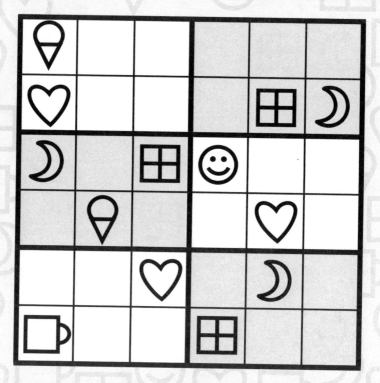

Solution on page 117

Solve the puzzle by using ◊, ☽, ⊞, ♡, ☺ or ☕.

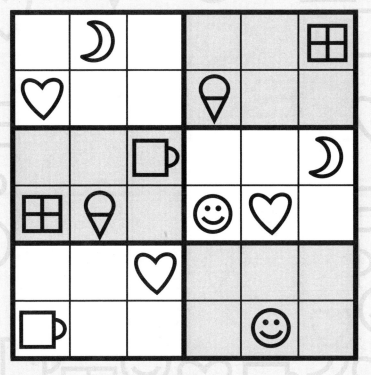

Solution on page 117

Solve the puzzle by using ♀, ☽, ⊞, ♡, ☺ or ⎕.

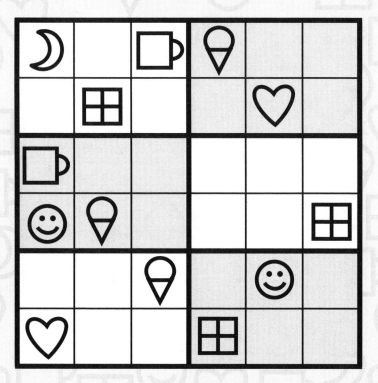

Solution on page 118

Solve the puzzle by using 💧, 🌙, ⊞, ♡, ☺ or ⊐.

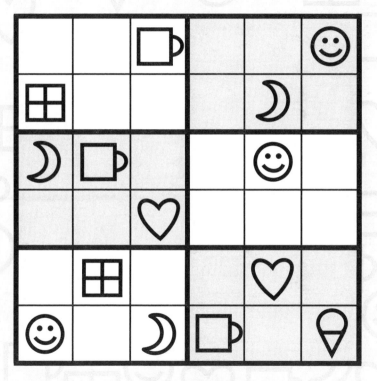

Solution on page 118

Solve the puzzle by using ♀, ☽, ⊞, ♡, ☺ or ☐.

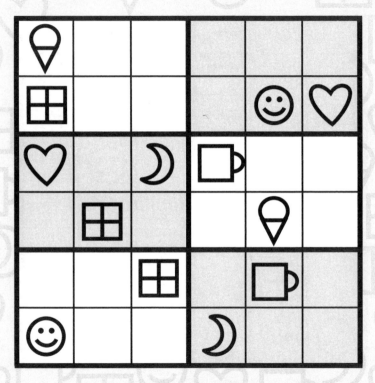

Solution on page 119

Solve the puzzle by using 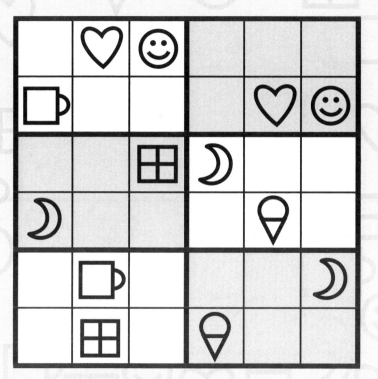, ☽, ⊞, ♡, ☺ or ☕.

Solution on page 119

Solve the puzzle by using ⏾,), ⊞, ♡, ☺ or ⃝.

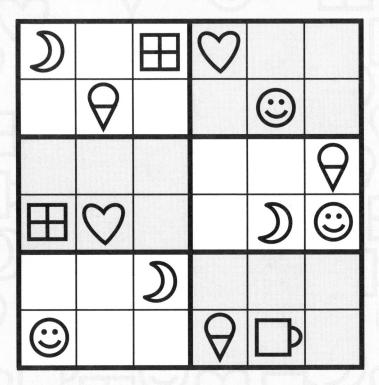

Solution on page 120

Solve the puzzle by using 📍, 🌙, ⊞, ♡, ☺ **or** ☕.

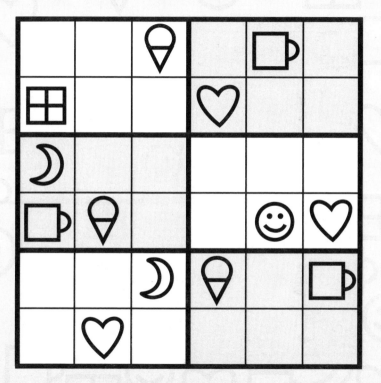

Solution on page 120

Solve the puzzle by using ♀, ☽, ⊞, ♡, ☺ or ☕.

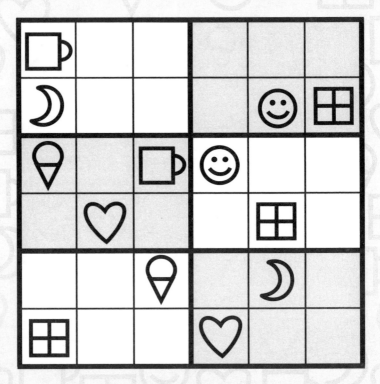

Solution on page 121

Solve the puzzle by using 💧, 🌙, ⊞, ♡, ☺ or 🍺.

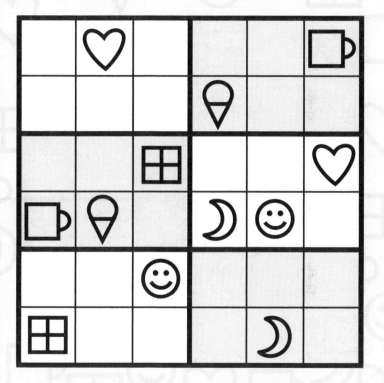

Solution on page 121

Solve the puzzle by using ♡, ☽, ⊞, ♡, ☺ or ⬠.

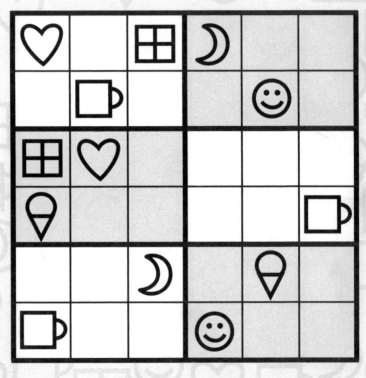

Solution on page 121

Solve the puzzle by using A, B, C, D, E or F.

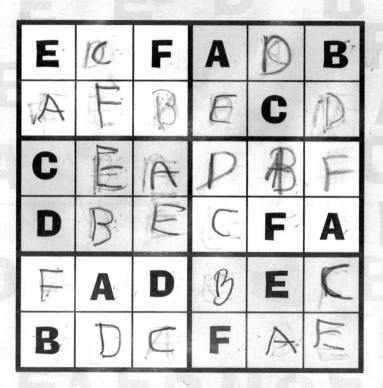

E	C	F	A	D	B
A	F	B	E	C	D
C	E	A	D	B	F
D	B	E	C	F	A
F	A	D	B	E	C
B	D	C	F	A	E

Solution on page 122

Solve the puzzle by using A, B, C, D, E or F.

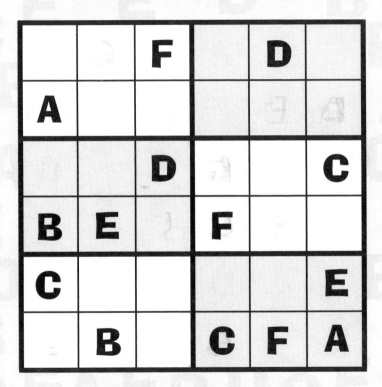

Solution on page 122

Solve the puzzle by using A, B, C, D, E or F.

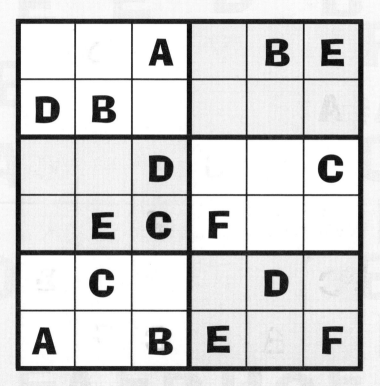

Solution on page 123

Solve the puzzle by using A, B, C, D, E or F.

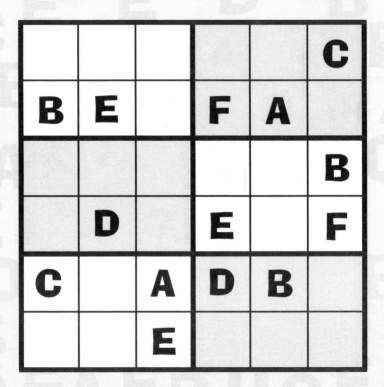

Solution on page 123

Solve the puzzle by using A, B, C, D, E or F.

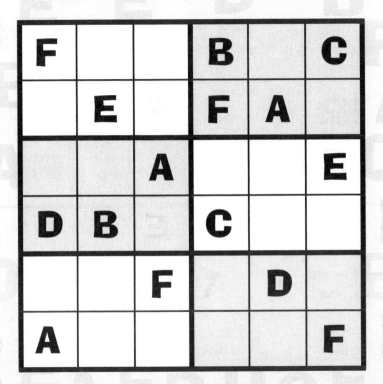

Solution on page 124

Solve the puzzle by using A, B, C, D, E or F.

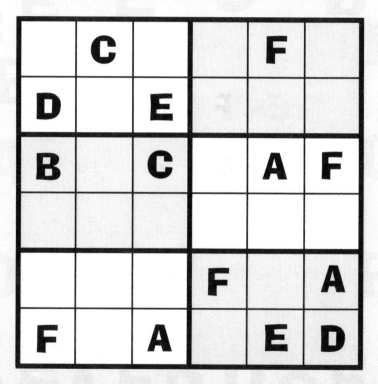

Solution on page 124

Solve the puzzle by using A, B, C, D, E or F.

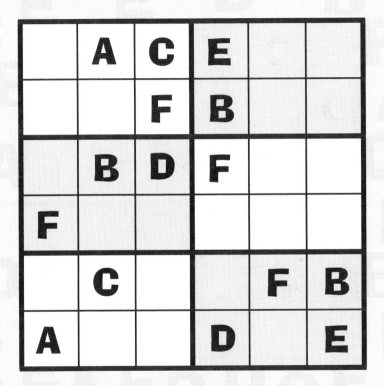

Solution on page 125

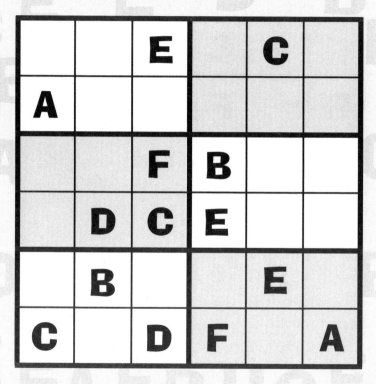

Solve the puzzle by using A, B, C, D, E or F.

		E		C	
A					
		F	B		
	D	C	E		
	B			E	
C		D	F		A

Solution on page125

Solve the puzzle by using A, B, C, D, E or F.

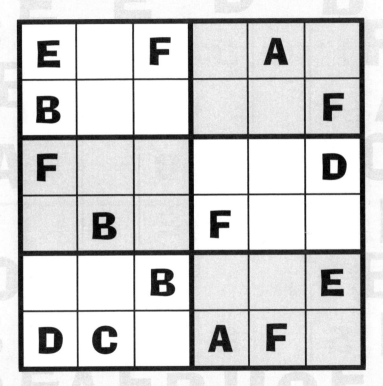

Solution on page 126

Solve the puzzle by using A, B, C, D, E or F.

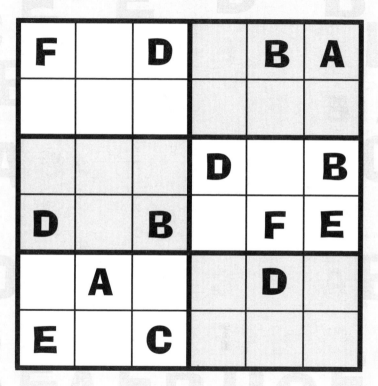

Solution on page 126

42

Solve the puzzle by using A, B, C, D, E or F.

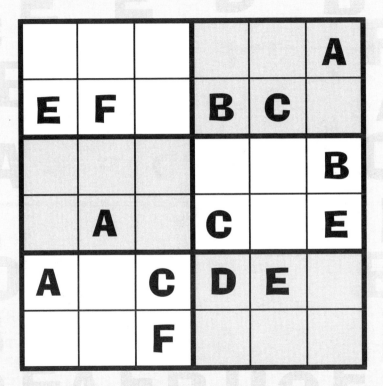

Solution on page 127

43

Solve the puzzle by using A, B, C, D, E or F.

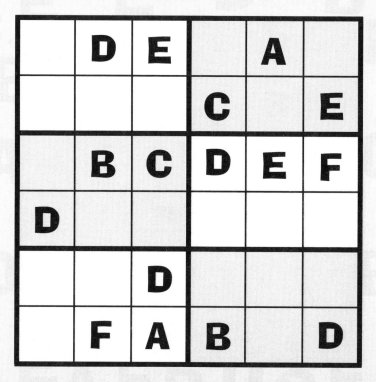

Solution on page 127

Solve the puzzle by using A, B, C, D, E or F.

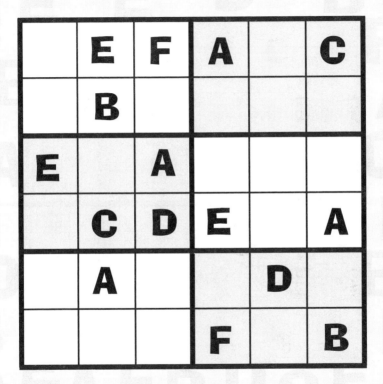

Solution on page 128

45

Solve the puzzle by using A, B, C, D, E or F.

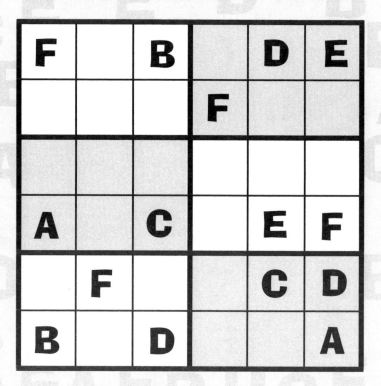

Solution on page 128

Solve the puzzle by using A, B, C, D, E or F.

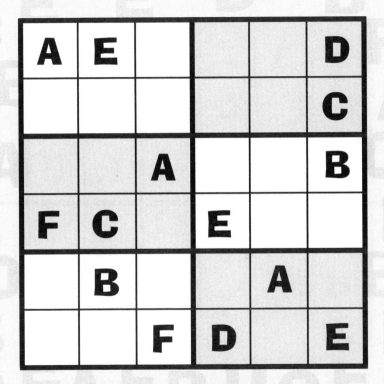

Solution on page 129

Solve the puzzle by using A, B, C, D, E or F.

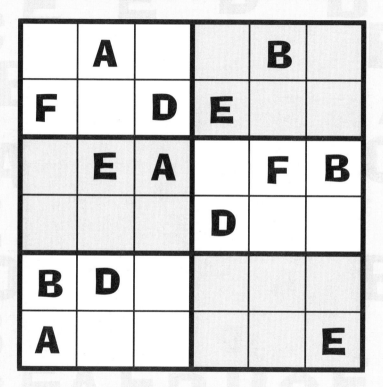

Solution on page 129

Solve the puzzle by using A, B, C, D, E or F.

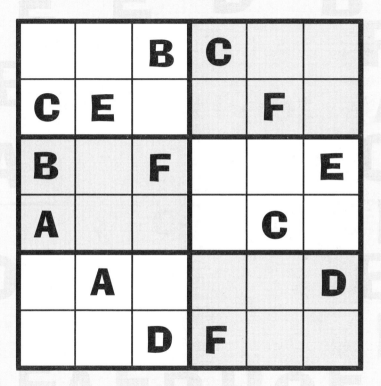

Solution on page 130

Solve the puzzle by using A, B, C, D, E or F.

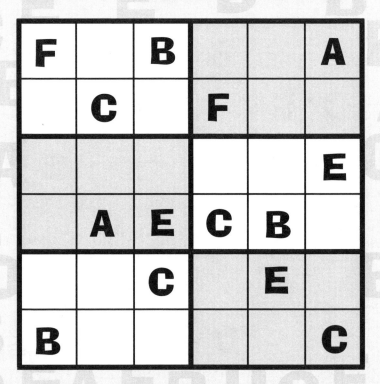

Solution on page 130

Solve the puzzle by using A, B, C, D, E or F.

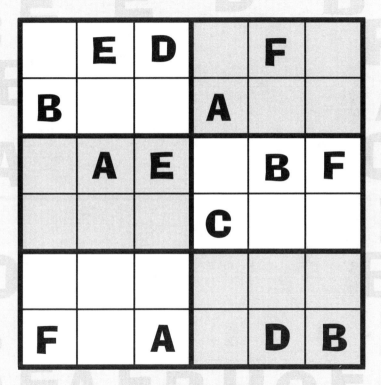

Solution on page 131

51

Solve the puzzle by using A, B, C, D, E or F.

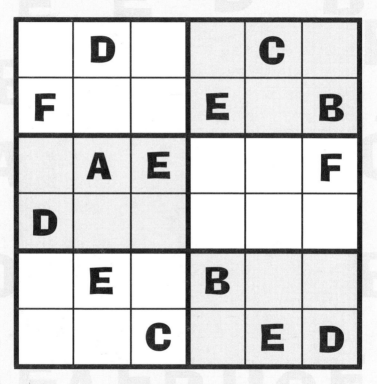

Solution on page 131

Solve the puzzle by using A, B, C, D, E or F.

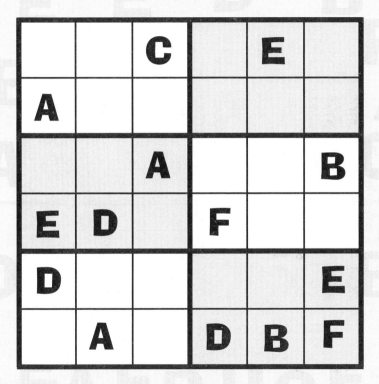

Solution on page 132

Solve the puzzle by using A, B, C, D, E or F.

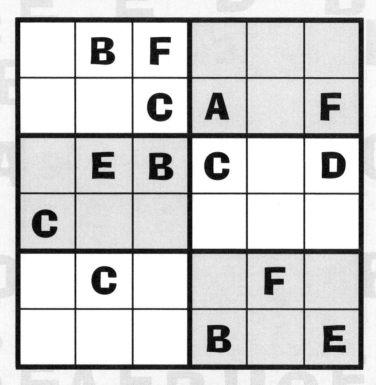

Solution on page 132

Solve the puzzle by using A, B, C, D, E or F.

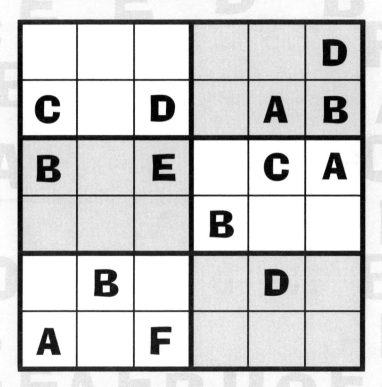

Solution on page 133

Solve the puzzle by using A, B, C, D, E or F.

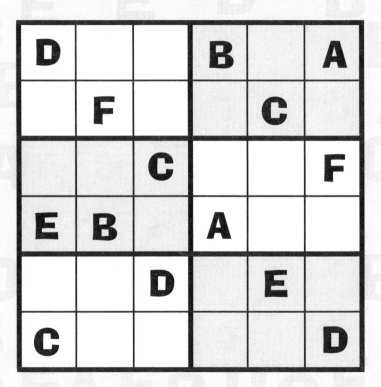

Solution on page 133

Solve the puzzle by using A, B, C, D, E or F.

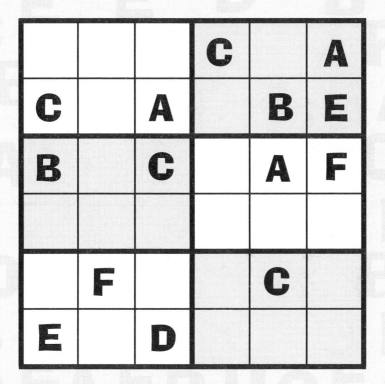

Solution on page 133

Solve the puzzle by using ○, □, ×, ◇, △ or ✛.

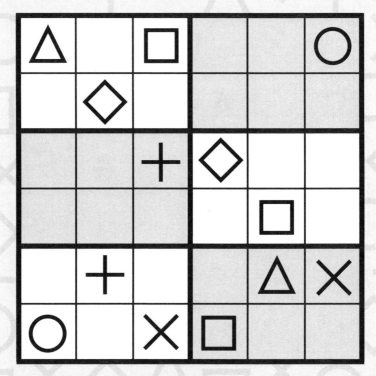

Solution on page 134

Solve the puzzle by using $\bigcirc$, $\square$, $\times$, $\diamondsuit$, $\triangle$ or $+$.

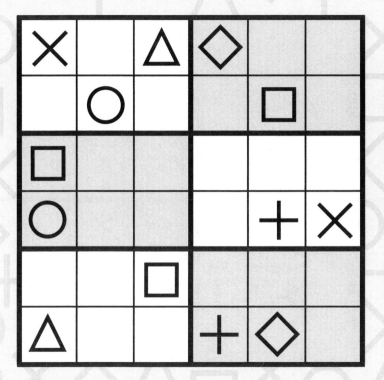

Solution on page 134

Solve the puzzle by using ◯, ▢, ✕, ◇, △ or ✛.

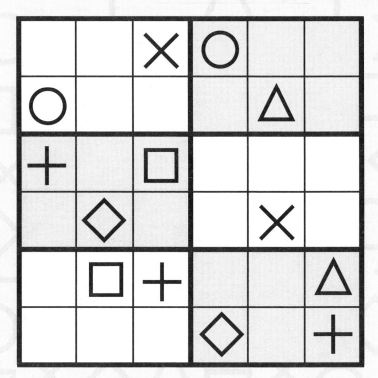

Solution on page 135

Solve the puzzle by using ○, □, ✕, ◇, △ or ✛.

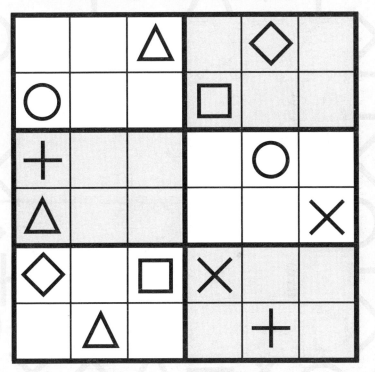

Solution on page 135

Solve the puzzle by using ○, □, ✕, ◇, △ or ┼.

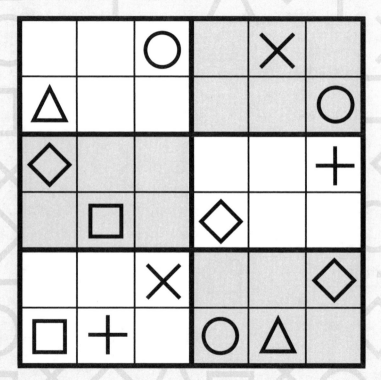

Solution on page 136

Solve the puzzle by using $\bigcirc$, $\square$, $\times$, $\diamondsuit$, $\triangle$ or $+$.

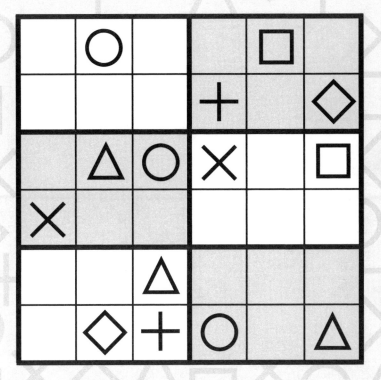

Solution on page 136

Solve the puzzle by using ◯, ▢, ✕, ◇, △ or ✚.

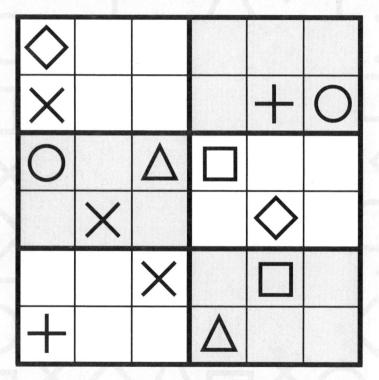

Solution on page 137

Solve the puzzle by using ○, □, ✕, ◇, △ or ✛.

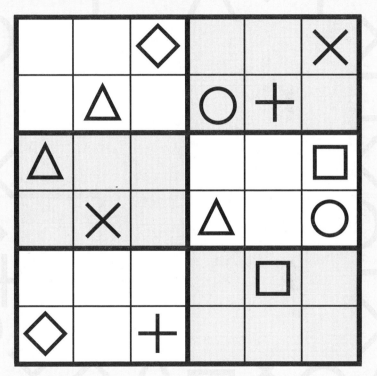

Solution on page 137

Solve the puzzle by using ○, □, ✕, ◇, △ or ✝.

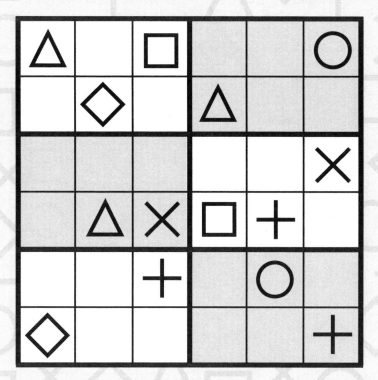

Solution on page 138

Solve the puzzle by using ◯, ▢, ✕, ◇, △ or ✛.

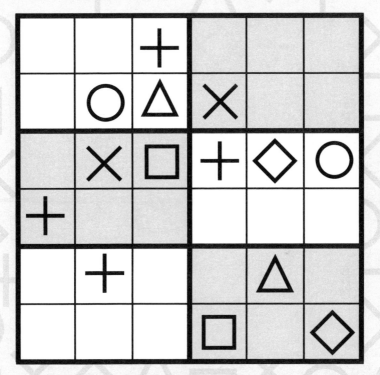

Solution on page 138

Solve the puzzle by using ○, □, ✕, ◇, △ or ✛.

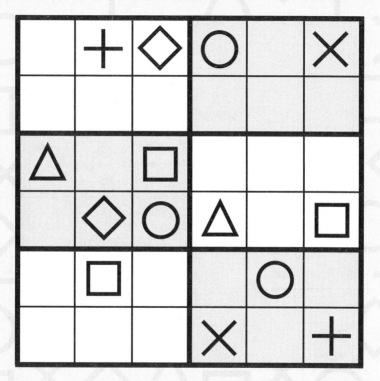

Solution on page 139

Solve the puzzle by using ○, □, ✕, ◇, △ or ✛.

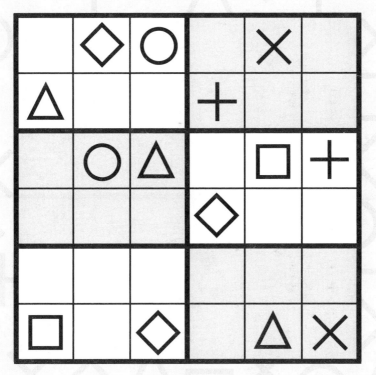

Solution on page 139

Solve the puzzle by using ○, □, ✕, ◇, △ or ✝.

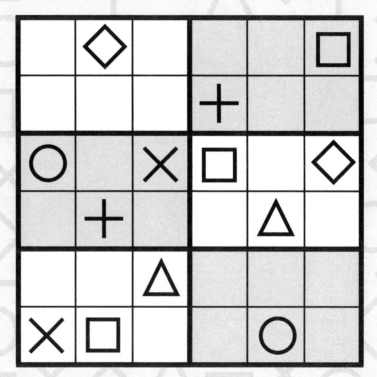

Solution on page 140

Solve the puzzle by using $\bigcirc$, $\square$, $\times$, $\diamondsuit$, $\triangle$ or $+$.

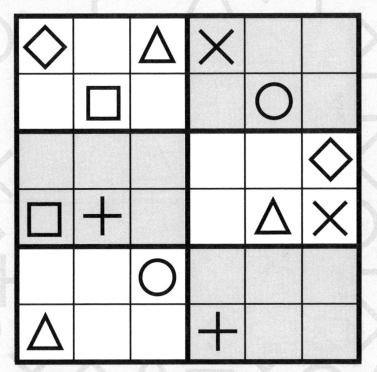

Solution on page 140

Solve the puzzle by using ○, □, ✕, ◇, △ or ✛.

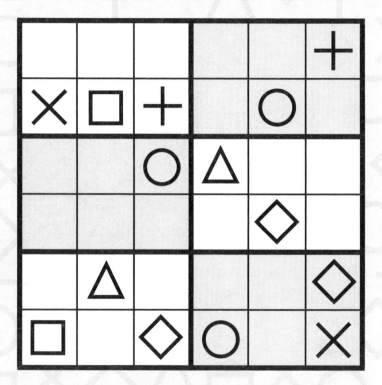

Solution on page 141

Solve the puzzle by using ◯, ▢, ✕, ◇, △ or ✛.

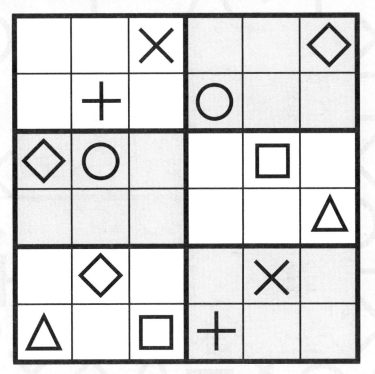

Solution on page 141

Solve the puzzle by using ○, □, ✕, ◇, △ or ✛.

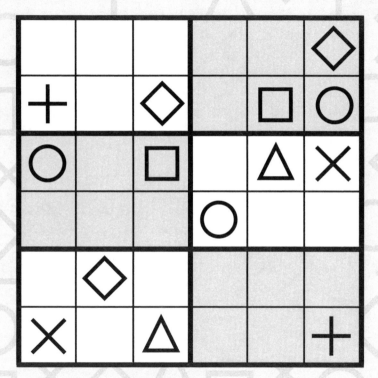

Solution on page 142

Solve the puzzle by using $\bigcirc$, $\square$, $\times$, $\diamondsuit$, $\triangle$ or $+$.

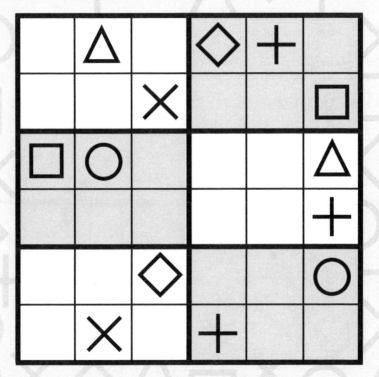

Solution on page 142

75

Solve the puzzle by using ○, □, ✕, ◇, △ or ✝.

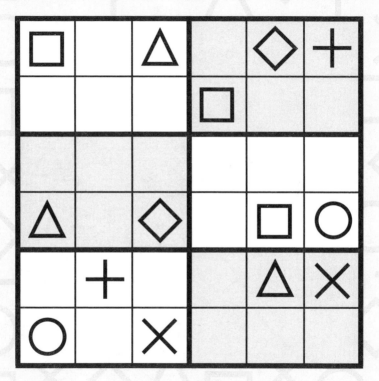

Solution on page 143

Solve the puzzle by using $\bigcirc$, $\square$, $\times$, $\diamondsuit$, $\triangle$ or $+$.

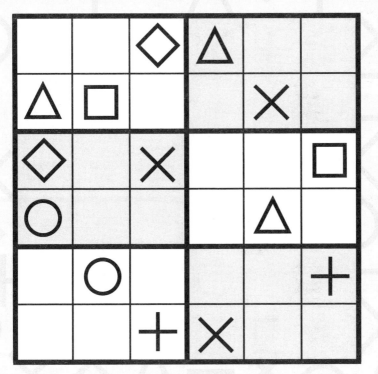

Solution on page 143

Solve the puzzle by using ○, □, ✕, ◇, △ or ✚.

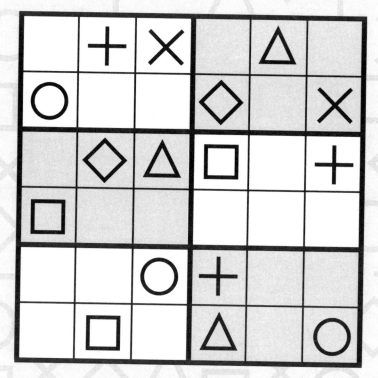

Solution on page 144

Solve the puzzle by using ○, □, ✕, ◇, △ or ✛.

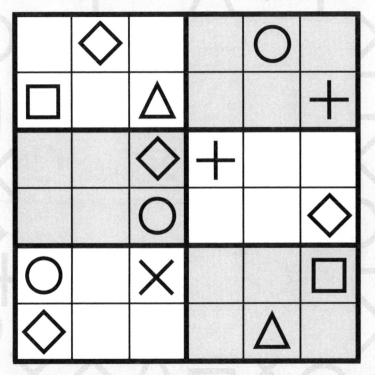

Solution on page 144

Solve the puzzle by using $\bigcirc$, $\square$, $\times$, $\diamond$, $\triangle$ **or** $+$.

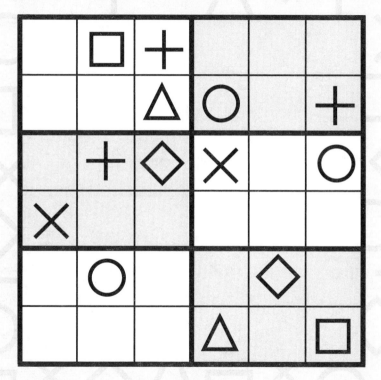

Solution on page 145

Solve the puzzle by using $\bigcirc$, $\square$, $\times$, $\diamondsuit$, $\triangle$ or $+$.

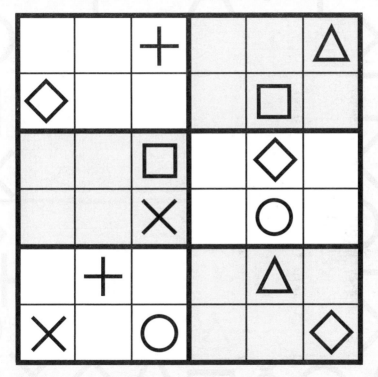

Solution on page 145

Solve the puzzle by using ○, □, ×, ◇, △ or +.

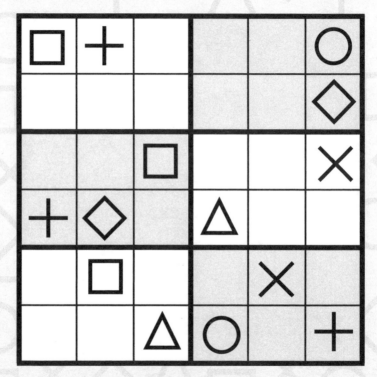

Solution on page 145

Solve the puzzle by using 1, 2, 3, 4, 5 or 6.

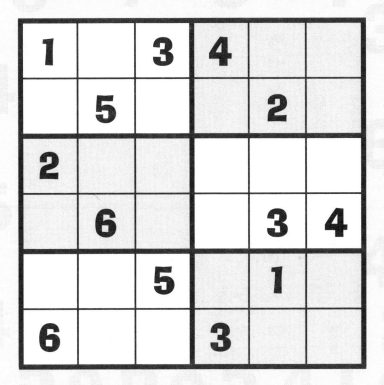

Solution on page 146

Solve the puzzle by using 1, 2, 3, 4, 5 or 6.

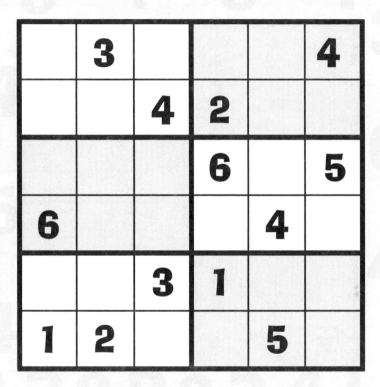

Solution on page 146

Solve the puzzle by using 1, 2, 3, 4, 5 or 6.

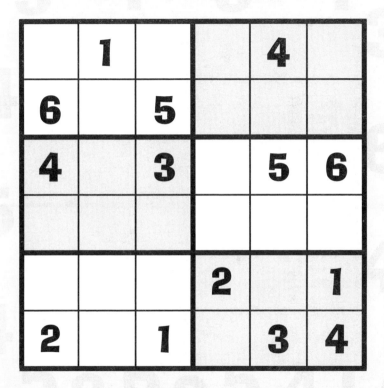

Solution on page 147

Solve the puzzle by using 1, 2, 3, 4, 5 or 6.

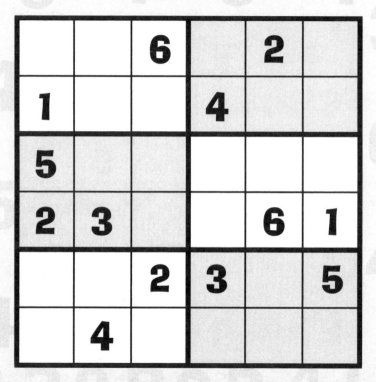

Solution on page 147

Solve the puzzle by using 1, 2, 3, 4, 5 or 6.

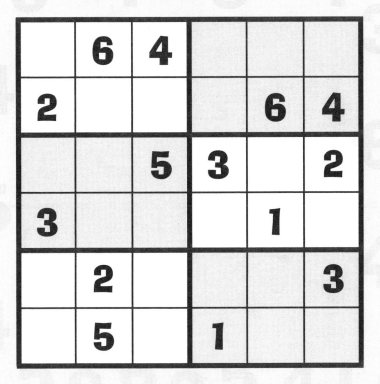

Solution on page 148

Solve the puzzle by using 1, 2, 3, 4, 5 or 6.

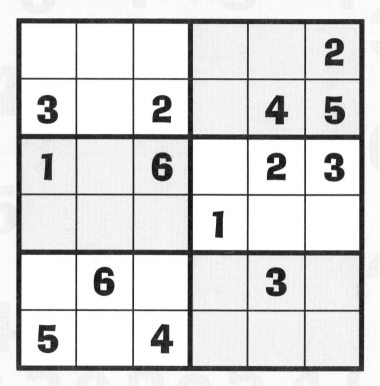

Solution on page 148

Solve the puzzle by using 1, 2, 3, 4, 5 or 6.

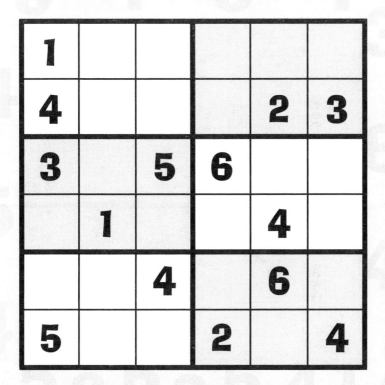

Solution on page 149

Solve the puzzle by using 1, 2, 3, 4, 5 or 6.

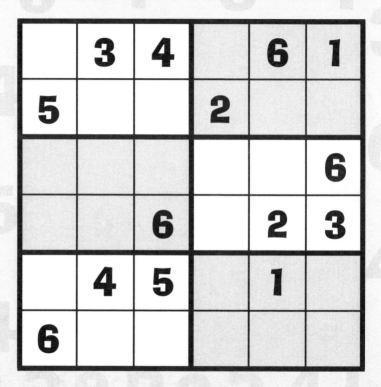

Solution on page149

Solve the puzzle by using 1, 2, 3, 4, 5 or 6.

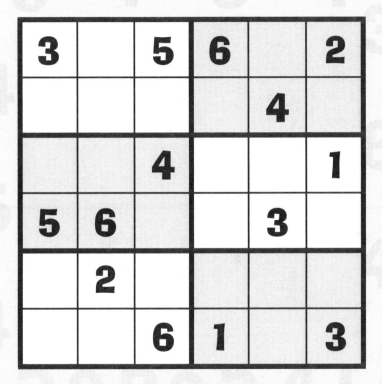

Solution on page 150

Solve the puzzle by using 1, 2, 3, 4, 5 or 6.

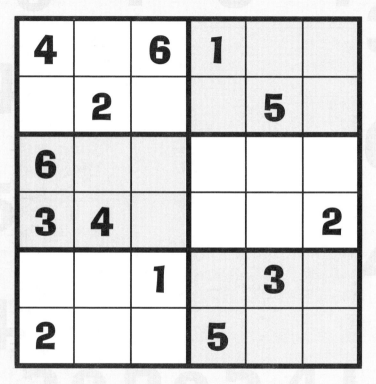

Solution on page 150

Solve the puzzle by using 1, 2, 3, 4, 5 or 6.

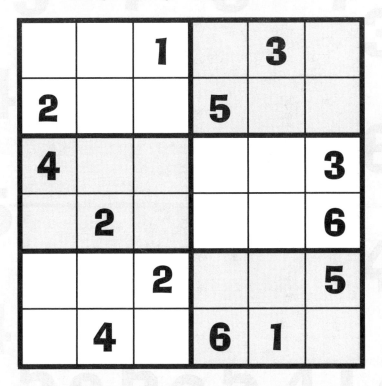

Solution on page 151

93

Solve the puzzle by using 1, 2, 3, 4, 5 or 6.

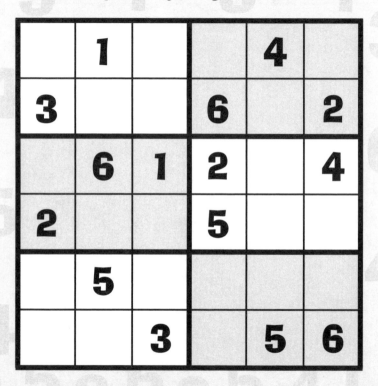

Solution on page 151

Solve the puzzle by using 1, 2, 3, 4, 5 or 6.

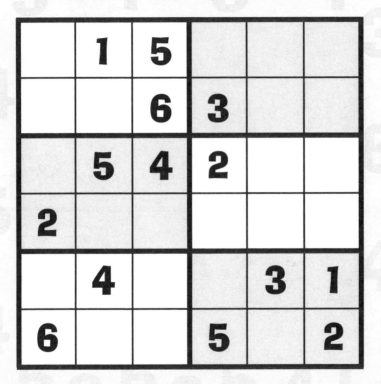

Solution on page 152

Solve the puzzle by using 1, 2, 3, 4, 5 or 6.

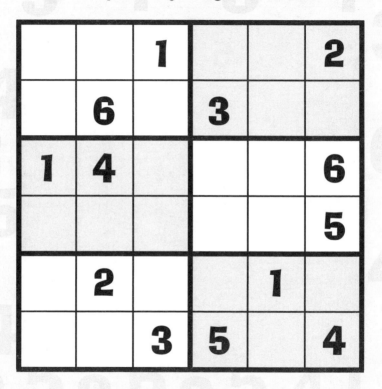

Solution on page 152

Solve the puzzle by using 1, 2, 3, 4, 5 or 6.

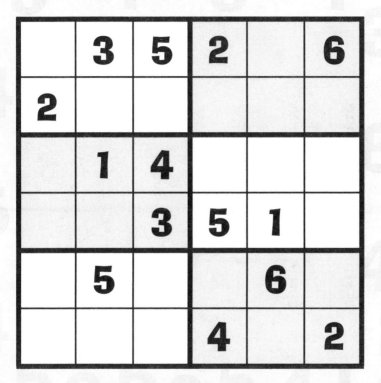

Solution on page 153

Solve the puzzle by using 1, 2, 3, 4, 5 or 6.

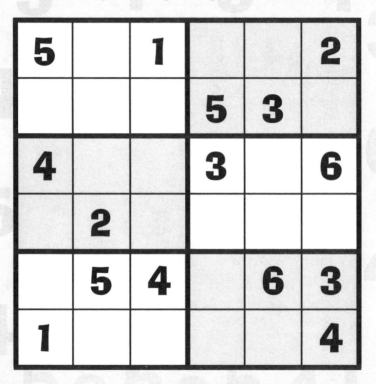

Solution on page153

Solve the puzzle by using 1, 2, 3, 4, 5 or 6.

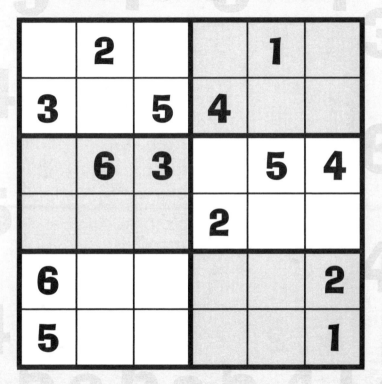

Solution on page 154

Solve the puzzle by using 1, 2, 3, 4, 5 or 6.

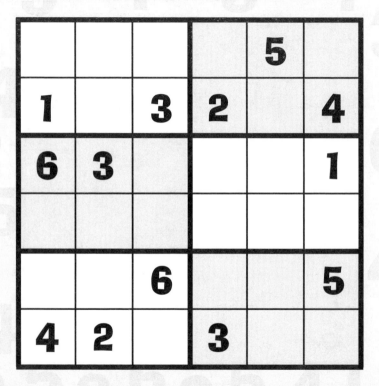

Solution on page154

Solve the puzzle by using 1, 2, 3, 4, 5 or 6.

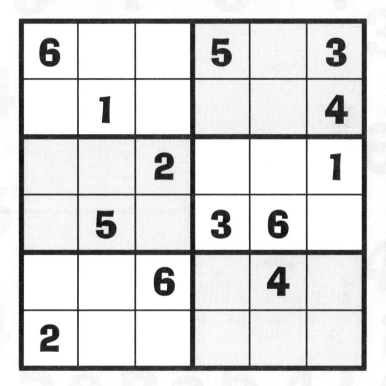

6			5		3
	1				4
		2			1
	5		3	6	
		6		4	
2					

Solution on page 155

Solve the puzzle by using 1, 2, 3, 4, 5 or 6.

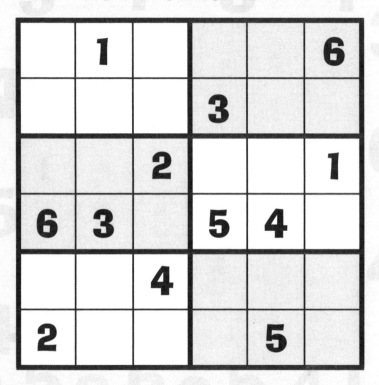

Solution on page155

Solve the puzzle by using 1, 2, 3, 4, 5 or 6.

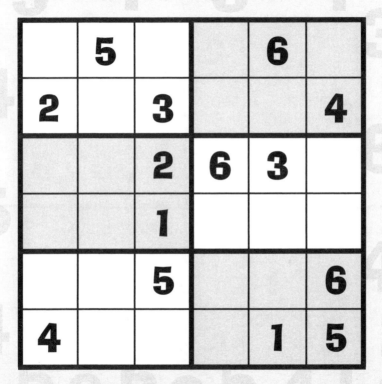

Solution on page 156

Solve the puzzle by using 1, 2, 3, 4, 5 or 6.

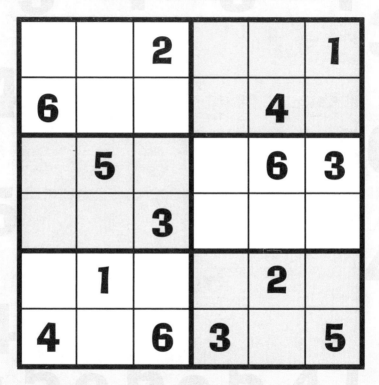

Solution on page 156

Solve the puzzle by using 1, 2, 3, 4, 5 or 6.

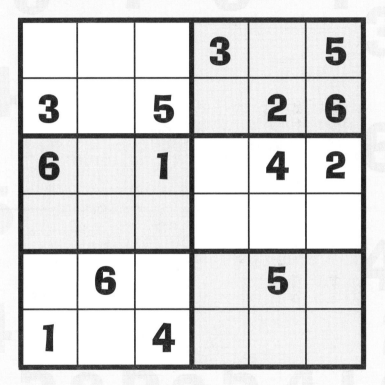

Solution on page 157

Solve the puzzle by using 1, 2, 3, 4, 5 or 6.

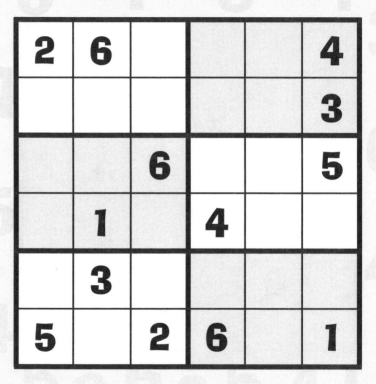

Solution on page 157

Solve the puzzle by using 1, 2, 3, 4, 5 or 6.

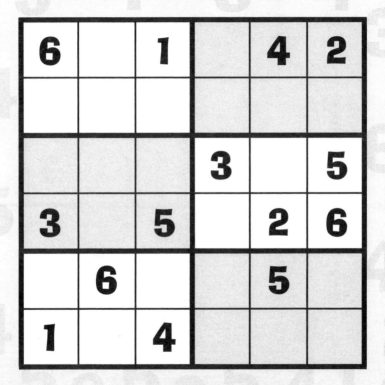

Solution on page 158

Solve the puzzle by using 1, 2, 3, 4, 5 or 6.

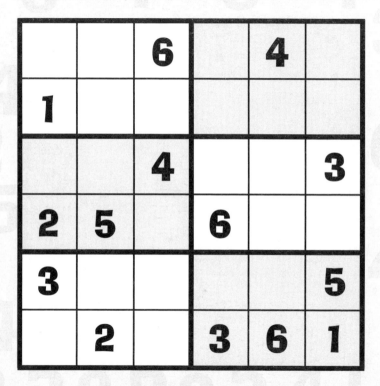

Solution on page 158

Solutions

Solutions

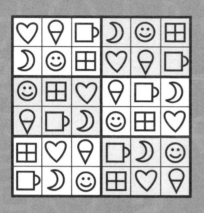

Page 8

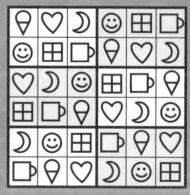

Page 9

Solutions

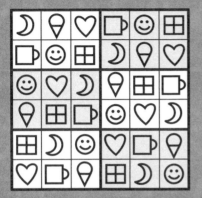

Page 10

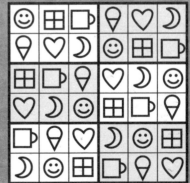

Page 11

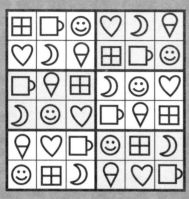

Page 12

Page 13

Solutions

Page 14

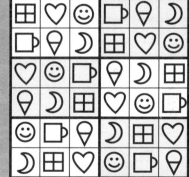

Page 15

Solutions

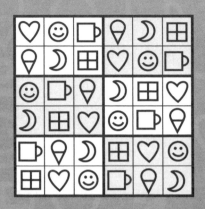

Page 16

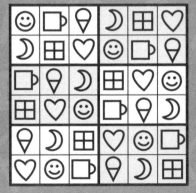

Page 17

Solutions

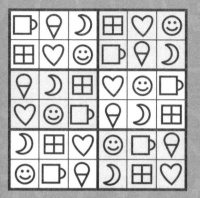

Page 18

Page 19

Solutions

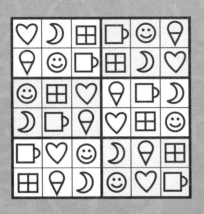

Page 20

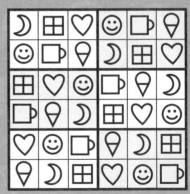

Page 21

Solutions

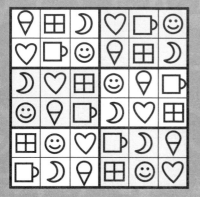

Page 22

Page 23

Solutions

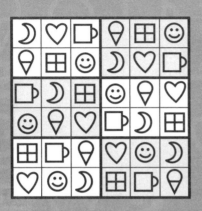

Page 24

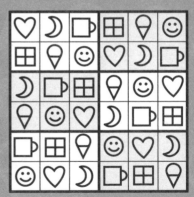

Page 25

Solutions

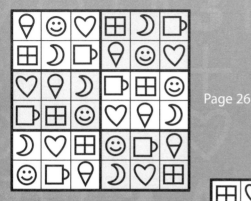

Page 26

Page 27

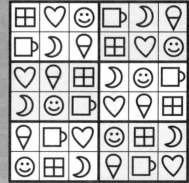

Solutions

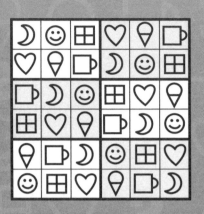

Page 28

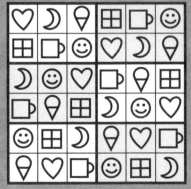

Page 29

Solutions

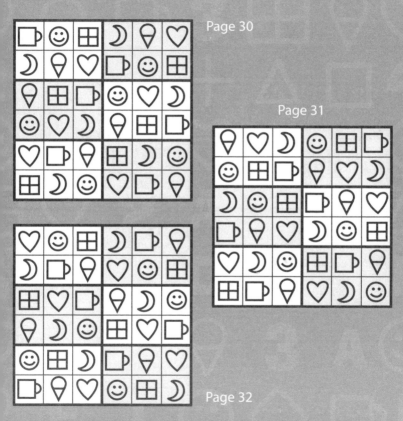

Page 30

Page 31

Page 32

Solutions

E	C	F	A	D	B
A	D	B	E	C	F
C	F	A	D	B	E
D	B	E	C	F	A
F	A	D	B	E	C
B	E	C	F	A	D

Page 33

E	C	F	A	D	B
A	D	B	E	C	F
F	A	D	B	E	C
B	E	C	F	A	D
C	F	A	D	B	E
D	B	E	C	F	A

Page 34

Solutions

C	F	A	D	B	E
D	B	E	C	F	A
F	A	D	B	E	C
B	E	C	F	A	D
E	C	F	A	D	B
A	D	B	E	C	F

Page 35

Page 36

F	A	D	B	E	C
B	E	C	F	A	D
E	C	F	A	D	B
A	D	B	E	C	F
C	F	A	D	B	E
D	B	E	C	F	A

Solutions

F	A	D	B	E	C
B	E	C	F	A	D
C	F	A	D	B	E
D	B	E	C	F	A
E	C	F	A	D	B
A	D	B	E	C	F

Page 37

Page38

A	C	B	D	F	E
D	F	E	A	C	B
B	D	C	E	A	F
E	A	F	B	D	C
C	E	D	F	B	A
F	B	A	C	E	D

Solutions

B	A	C	E	D	F
E	D	F	B	A	C
C	B	D	F	E	A
F	E	A	C	B	D
D	C	E	A	F	B
A	F	B	D	C	E

Page 39

Page 40

D	F	E	A	C	B
A	C	B	D	F	E
E	A	F	B	D	C
B	D	C	E	A	F
F	B	A	C	E	D
C	E	D	F	B	A

Solutions

E	D	F	B	A	C
B	A	C	E	D	F
F	E	A	C	B	D
C	B	D	F	E	A
A	F	B	D	C	E
D	C	E	A	F	B

Page 41

Page 42

F	E	D	C	B	A
C	B	A	F	E	D
A	F	E	D	C	B
D	C	B	A	F	E
B	A	F	E	D	C
E	D	C	B	A	F

Solutions

B	C	D	E	F	A
E	F	A	B	C	D
C	D	E	F	A	B
F	A	B	C	D	E
A	B	C	D	E	F
D	E	F	A	B	C

Page 43

Page 44

C	D	E	F	A	B
F	A	B	C	D	E
A	B	C	D	E	F
D	E	F	A	B	C
B	C	D	E	F	A
E	F	A	B	C	D

Solutions

D	E	F	A	B	C
A	B	C	D	E	F
E	F	A	B	C	D
B	C	D	E	F	A
F	A	B	C	D	E
C	D	E	F	A	B

Page 45

Page 46

F	A	B	C	D	E
C	D	E	F	A	B
D	E	F	A	B	C
A	B	C	D	E	F
E	F	A	B	C	D
B	C	D	E	F	A

Solutions

A	E	C	B	F	D
B	F	D	A	E	C
E	D	A	F	C	B
F	C	B	E	D	A
D	B	E	C	A	F
C	A	F	D	B	E

Page 47

E	A	C	F	B	D
F	B	D	E	A	C
D	E	A	C	F	B
C	F	B	D	E	A
B	D	E	A	C	F
A	C	F	B	D	E

Page 48

Solutions

D	F	B	C	E	A
C	E	A	D	F	B
B	C	F	A	D	E
A	D	E	B	C	F
F	A	C	E	B	D
E	B	D	F	A	C

Page 49

Page 50

F	D	B	E	C	A
E	C	A	F	D	B
C	B	F	D	A	E
D	A	E	C	B	F
A	F	C	B	E	D
B	E	D	A	F	C

Solutions

A	E	D	B	F	C
B	F	C	A	E	D
C	A	E	D	B	F
D	B	F	C	A	E
E	D	B	F	C	A
F	C	A	E	D	B

Page 51

Page 52

E	D	B	F	C	A
F	C	A	E	D	B
C	A	E	D	B	F
D	B	F	C	A	E
A	E	D	B	F	C
B	F	C	A	E	D

Solutions

B	F	C	A	E	D
A	E	D	B	F	C
F	C	A	E	D	B
E	D	B	F	C	A
D	B	F	C	A	E
C	A	E	D	B	F

Page 53

A	B	F	E	D	C
E	D	C	A	B	F
F	E	B	C	A	D
C	A	D	F	E	B
B	C	E	D	F	A
D	F	A	B	C	E

Page 54

Solutions

Page 55

F	A	B	C	E	D
C	E	D	F	A	B
B	F	E	D	C	A
D	C	A	B	F	E
E	B	C	A	D	F
A	D	F	E	B	C

Page 56

D	C	E	B	F	A
B	F	A	D	C	E
A	D	C	E	B	F
E	B	F	A	D	C
F	A	D	C	E	B
C	E	B	F	A	D

F	B	E	C	D	A
C	D	A	F	B	E
B	E	C	D	A	F
D	A	F	B	E	C
A	F	B	E	C	D
E	C	D	A	F	B

Page 57

Solutions

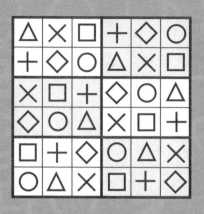

Page 58

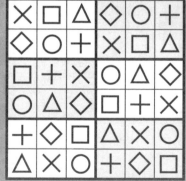

Page 59

Solutions

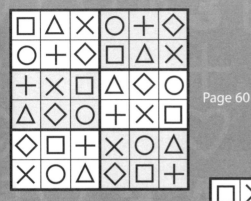

Page 60

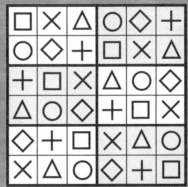

Page 61

Solutions

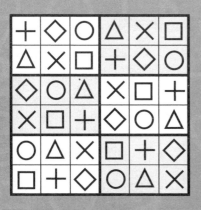

Page 62

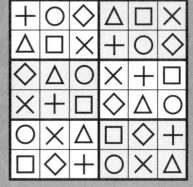

Page 63

Solutions

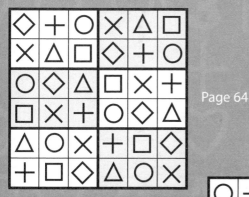

Page 64

Page 65

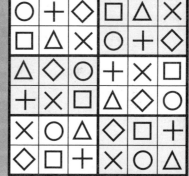

Solutions

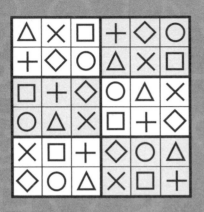

Page 66

Page 67

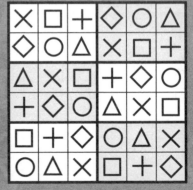

Solutions

Page 68

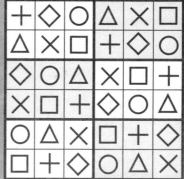

Page 69

Solutions

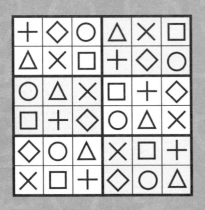

Page 70

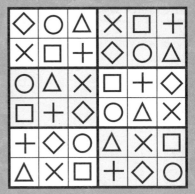

Page 71

Solutions

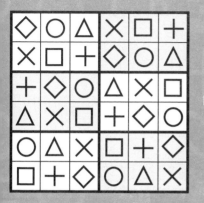

Page 72

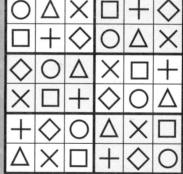

Page 73

Solutions

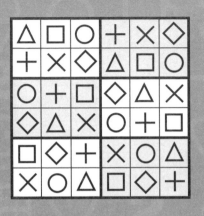

Page 74

Page 75

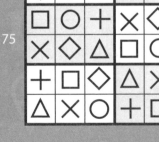

Solutions

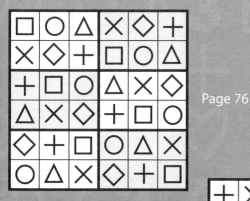

Page 76

Page 77

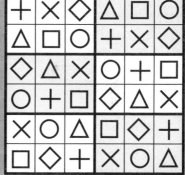

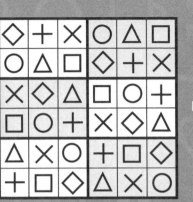

Solutions

Page 78

Page 79

Solutions

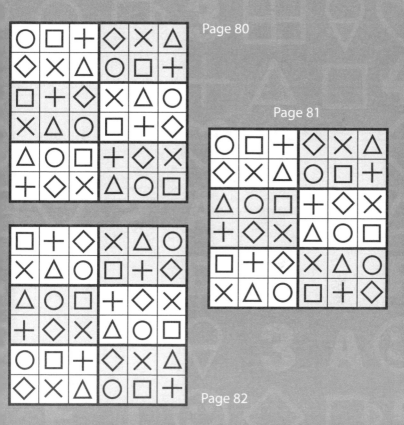

Page 80

Page 81

Page 82

Solutions

1	2	3	4	5	6
4	5	6	1	2	3
2	3	4	5	6	1
5	6	1	2	3	4
3	4	5	6	1	2
6	1	2	3	4	5

Page 83

Page 84

2	3	1	5	6	4
5	6	4	2	3	1
3	4	2	6	1	5
6	1	5	3	4	2
4	5	3	1	2	6
1	2	6	4	5	3

Solutions

3	1	2	6	4	5
6	4	5	3	1	2
4	2	3	1	5	6
1	5	6	4	2	3
5	3	4	2	6	1
2	6	1	5	3	4

Page 85

Page 86

4	5	6	1	2	3
1	2	3	4	5	6
5	6	1	2	3	4
2	3	4	5	6	1
6	1	2	3	4	5
3	4	5	6	1	2

Solutions

5	6	4	2	3	1
2	3	1	5	6	4
6	1	5	3	4	2
3	4	2	6	1	5
1	2	6	4	5	3
4	5	3	1	2	6

Page 87

Page 88

6	4	5	3	1	2
3	1	2	6	4	5
1	5	6	4	2	3
4	2	3	1	5	6
2	6	1	5	3	4
5	3	4	2	6	1

Solutions

1	2	3	4	5	6
4	5	6	1	2	3
3	4	5	6	1	2
6	1	2	3	4	5
2	3	4	5	6	1
5	6	1	2	3	4

Page 89

Page 90

2	3	4	5	6	1
5	6	1	2	3	4
1	2	3	4	5	6
4	5	6	1	2	3
3	4	5	6	1	2
6	1	2	3	4	5

Solutions

3	4	5	6	1	2
6	1	2	3	4	5
2	3	4	5	6	1
5	6	1	2	3	4
1	2	3	4	5	6
4	5	6	1	2	3

Page 91

Page 92

4	5	6	1	2	3
1	2	3	4	5	6
6	1	2	3	4	5
3	4	5	6	1	2
5	6	1	2	3	4
2	3	4	5	6	1

Solutions

5	6	1	2	3	4
2	3	4	5	6	1
4	5	6	1	2	3
1	2	3	4	5	6
6	1	2	3	4	5
3	4	5	6	1	2

Page 93

Page 94

6	1	2	3	4	5
3	4	5	6	1	2
5	6	1	2	3	4
2	3	4	5	6	1
4	5	6	1	2	3
1	2	3	4	5	6

Solutions

3	1	5	4	2	6
4	2	6	3	1	5
1	5	4	2	6	3
2	6	3	1	5	4
5	4	2	6	3	1
6	3	1	5	4	2

Page 95

Page 96

3	5	1	4	6	2
4	6	2	3	5	1
1	4	5	2	3	6
2	3	6	1	4	5
5	2	4	6	1	3
6	1	3	5	2	4

Solutions

1	3	5	2	4	6
2	4	6	1	3	5
5	1	4	6	2	3
6	2	3	5	1	4
4	5	2	3	6	1
3	6	1	4	5	2

Page 97

Page 98

5	3	1	6	4	2
6	4	2	5	3	1
4	1	5	3	2	6
3	2	6	4	1	5
2	5	4	1	6	3
1	6	3	2	5	4

Solutions

4	2	6	3	1	5
3	1	5	4	2	6
2	6	3	1	5	4
1	5	4	2	6	3
6	3	1	5	4	2
5	4	2	6	3	1

Page 99

Page 100

2	6	4	1	5	3
1	5	3	2	6	4
6	3	2	5	4	1
5	4	1	6	3	2
3	1	6	4	2	5
4	2	5	3	1	6

Solutions

6	2	4	5	1	3
5	1	3	6	2	4
3	6	2	4	5	1
4	5	1	3	6	2
1	3	6	2	4	5
2	4	5	1	3	6

Page 101

Page 102

3	1	5	4	2	6
4	2	6	3	1	5
5	4	2	6	3	1
6	3	1	5	4	2
1	5	4	2	6	3
2	6	3	1	5	4

Solutions

1	5	4	2	6	3
2	6	3	1	5	4
5	4	2	6	3	1
6	3	1	5	4	2
3	1	5	4	2	6
4	2	6	3	1	5

Page 103

5	4	2	6	3	1
6	3	1	5	4	2
1	5	4	2	6	3
2	6	3	1	5	4
3	1	5	4	2	6
4	2	6	3	1	5

Page 104

Solutions

4	2	6	3	1	5
3	1	5	4	2	6
6	3	1	5	4	2
5	4	2	6	3	1
2	6	3	1	5	4
1	5	4	2	6	3

Page 105

Page 106

2	6	3	1	5	4
1	5	4	2	6	3
4	2	6	3	1	5
3	1	5	4	2	6
6	3	1	5	4	2
5	4	2	6	3	1

Solutions

6	3	1	5	4	2
5	4	2	6	3	1
4	2	6	3	1	5
3	1	5	4	2	6
2	6	3	1	5	4
1	5	4	2	6	3

Page 107

Page 108

5	3	6	1	4	2
1	4	2	5	3	6
6	1	4	2	5	3
2	5	3	6	1	4
3	6	1	4	2	5
4	2	5	3	6	1